THE TREES
THE TREES

Also by Heather Christle:

The Difficult Farm (Octopus Books 2009)
What is Amazing (Wesleyan University Press 2012)

THE TREES
THE TREES

BY HEATHER CHRISTLE

OCTOPUS BOOKS
PORTLAND/DENVER/OMAHA

OCTOPUS
BOOKS

The Trees The Trees
© Heather Christle

First Edition, 2011
Second Edition, 2012
ISBN: 978-0-9801938-7-9
Printed & Bound in the USA

Cover design by Denny Schmickle
www.dennyschmickle.com

Layout design by Emma Barnett
www.therealemmabarnett.com

Octopus Books 2011
Portland/Denver/Omaha
www.octopusbooks.net

For Chris

CONTENTS

I don't care
about the flowers, which I merely invented
to give myself another reason to address you.

—Aleksandar Ristović

THAT AIR OF RUTHLESSNESS IN SPRING

here is the hand   here is the hand   on my face
it's not my hand   it's a beautiful day   again   I
can hardly believe anything   what about you who
are so frequently touching   some part of the world
what is it you're touching today   when I touch the
trees   the trees think *man-child*   they are so
wrong   but it is a human face I put on   I am
hung up under this weather   I am hanging on tight
to a swing   when I go up enough I jump   then I
am not touching anything   then the world thinks
I've disappeared   I am just having a little fun
not much fun at all   are you sad   did you touch
the world   the wrong way   everything is always
happening   and not just for show   I want to
show you something   I don't care what   I want
you to look where I say

YOU ARE MY GUEST

I will call you man   man man man man   it is a
recipe   it is not that expensive   I will have you
over for dinner   and I will not take your clothes
off   you wear clothes like a man man   you are a
tightly wound bundle   when we think of the
woods   the woods are the same   but the rabbit
between them is different   eat up your soup
little man   little man man   there is no food
coming later

JE M'APPELLE IVAN

I am alone   I am a real bear   with a head full of
hazard and light   I live in nature   live with no
friends   and no equity   who needs it   I have
my face   I have my hands   which are as I speak
mauling the air   one time I took a trip   I lay
horizontal on a marvelous raft   I did look up
regard the blank stars   and accept them as holes in
the frame   one time I ran so fast   I left my own
self behind   my own self wandered into an old
birch   and it fell over   I have no escrow   O
bees thou sweet kingdom of noise   I worship
freely   I pee on the leaves   and the wind
impulses right through me   like a small clean rock
all I want is the fish to glow at night   when
everyone on earth is trying to reach me   *hello*
yes *hello*   this never happens   yet other events
go on and on   the dimming of the moon   I am
upright   I am lumbering   alone with no liquidity
and I live on berries   deliver me berries   if later
on you glide   into these wild and wilder woods

HALF-HEDGEHOG HALF-MAN

talk to me   I said   *okay*   said the tree   and it
twinkled   *not like that*   I said   *I already know*
that   *talk to me about something new*   *you*
monster   it said   that was a little better   *could*
we try this   I said   *from a different perspective*
so we swapped places   I was still the monster
this would be easier   if you could see the video
in the video   there are all these owls   like bang
bang bang   all over the tree   which I was now
only that might be clearer in writing   because I
was also still myself   half-hedgehog   half-man
and that could be hard   to communicate visually
and also my man-face was glass

THAT LITTLE BIRD WAS NOT OKAY

I have been hiding for two hours   behind your
idea of a theme park   one giant teacup and a fence
nobody wants to tell you   you are the top general
on the losing side   of a war I started before I could
speak   babies communicate with each other
using shadows and casual tumbles   I love your
body   I have to weep   every day   I don't know
why   it doesn't help the flowers grow any faster
speed concerns me   speed considers itself   so
lightly   it doesn't look like thinking   it looks like
a tangerine   how many times   will I blink
between now   and the moment you find me   not
here   I hope   some place   I haven't imagined   it
is a lark   to love your face so much   and from
a minimum distance   of ten to fifteen feet

I HIGHLIGHTED YOUR PARTS

life is very easy   you just have to memorize it   in
advance   like this morning   you put on your
watch   the wrong way for a moment   that was a
brilliant stroke   so small   so human   you just
have to know your behavior   and execute it   like
love   like reaching down to pick up a bullet   and
then no one ever tells you   where it's from
everything lies down and waits its turn   this house
the van   the mast   your private kidney   it's
March 18   a Tuesday   right away the phone
neglects to ring

ANYWHERE IN PARTICULAR

I will leave this house   and go out into the weather
there are only so many ways to get out   I will use
the window as a shield   and nothing can hurt me
not rain   not migration   I need a truck   I need
to drive forever down the highway   carrying
nothing   going out to meet the owls   *hello owls*
on a man-made hill   *hello men*   you dead men
beneath a separate weather   and now I am back in
the truck   reliable   plain   I could drive across
Nebraska   and no one would notice   I don't need
to hide at all anymore   something in the night sky
changed   so slightly   I have to pay attention
and yes   their mouths are ahead of the sound
there is no one to tell   I tell the truck   I tell
Nebraska I am leaving   that there are a million
ways out   one day I will live   on an island   all
the time   I will send out a parcel   when the mail
boat arrives   *look empty mail boat   now you are
full*

MY ENEMY

I have a new enemy   he is so good-looking   here
is a photograph   of him in the snow   he is in the
snow   and so is the photo   I put it there because
I hate him   and because it is always snowing   in
the photograph   my enemy is acting   like there
are no neighbors   but there are always neighbors
they just might be far away   he is 100% evil
and good-looking   he looks good   in his parka
in the snow   if you asked   he would call it a
helmet   all he ever does is lie   he does not
breathe   or move   or glow   he is not that kind
of man   it is not that kind of snow

THESE PEOPLE ARE GETTING TOGETHER

a woman and a man are on a bench   the bench is
vibrating   and the trees and purses   that which
does not vibrate falls apart   the dead also vibrate
the woman and the man are still alive I think   I
know a lot about the world   when the man says he
will fix dinner   he does not mean he will repair it
and winning is one object of the sun   there is no
good way to draw smoke   compared to smoke
the bench is real life   real life keeps hills piled up
behind it   a bench is in memory of the dead
sometimes a choice is needed   to pick the door
and not the doorway   the woman makes an offer
the man forgets to vibrate   and promptly falls
apart

A HANDLE ON IT

I was born into a bandit family   it's not like I had
any choice   or like I have ever helped anyone
anywhere   must have filled in a dozen coloring
book tidepools as a kid   and touched starfish
constantly   can't believe I had time for anything
else   I am trying to make a story about myself
and a whale   and I am trying to understand a
house   from the nailgun's perspective   I had to
spend months in a drawer   getting out is
spectacular   where would you like to go   we can
go until there's no money left anywhere   and we
have developed more interesting hair   right now I
have a feeling   like I am some very good
embroidery   I'd like you to hang me up   behind
the sofa   so I could watch you make friends with
your guests   and at night have time alone   to
unravel   to start over   with my big tree shifted
one inch to the left

AND YET I'M NOT A TREE

I have no relatives   I can't move   therefore I am
covered in snow   my inability to speak has saved
me   from attending endless parties   among my
friends I count the window   opportunities
surround me   and fame   the famous sidewalk
the famous building   everything is fine   I do not
possess a license   in this state   or any   I'd like
to cry out *any* in my sleep   I never do   never
sleep   never turn around to watch the chimney   I
do not know how to hold a rifle   what birds have
for me   is not respect

PROMOTION

it is hard to be angry with you   while levitating
five inches off the floor   I have achieved
something   I am two days old   a cat   I don't
look like anything yet   some skin   it is
impossible for you to be angry with me   I hope
if it is September   you go to fetch apples   and I
am not matching leaves in a tree   levitating five
inches off the tree   it's redundant   but that never
stopped the clouds   I'm napping on the television
two days old   and already I have seen nothing
through a window   I am not interested   in how
one thing changes another   for example   you are
feeding me   and also you keep feeding me   so in
one or two ways I am bigger

WHEN THE SUN WENT DOWN THEY KEPT GROWING

now I understand   you are the owner of a small
piece of time   like anyone else   tonight
everyone's sending me flowers   and I am upset
thinking maybe where I am the earth will collapse
I mean   they are light enough   but gather this
many together   and some are peonies   I can't
understand how they even stand up   babies can't
do what they do   I don't want to be over   any
time in the next hundred years   on the night of the
one thousand migrating geese   they were hiding
the whole goddamn lake   if you can imagine   of
course you can   you are not some mindless phlox
and Amanda listen   because this affects us both
your wind-chimes sound adorable   when I come
in they injure my head

PLOT THE HEIGHT AND DISTANCE

now you have gone and died again   you were my
family   I am up here   in this tree   it is not
impossible   I can still see you   you are two
buoys out there in the bay   are you waving at me
do you miss me   when I move I shake the tree
and no other part   that is polite   are you damp
are you salty   my family   you are so orange   so
much a pair and rooting for caution   I have fallen
out of my tree   and the tree is still shaking   it
was not me making things happen   I watch a gull
fly through the sky the tree circumscribes   why
not say that it flew right into my eye   a pain can
arrive from anywhere   except the bay   you are in
the bay and watching   you are my family   I want
two rowboats   one below   one to cover me from
rain   I saw a cloud coming in   the air is changing
the cloud flew right into my eye   and did not hurt
me

THE WHOLE THING IS THE HARD PART

you have to live where the house lands on you
what else can you do   your bones are all broken
and somebody loves you   who is it   tell me who
loves you   not as much as I do   I mean   I even
built you a house   and found you   why won't
you live in it

POEM ENDING WITH SOME ADVICE

I want to live in the rectangle   it lights me up   I
swear   it is nothing I have ever seen before
reject this season   I said to myself   and fucked it
out of existence   thank you for coming   I am
happy to see you   it is nice to see you   from
across the prophylactic lake   here is my advice
if you want to make a commercial   about two
tortoises with internet trouble   their house should
be a one-story ranch   if you want people to   you
know   believe you

INDOORS THE GREAT

if I silently praise my enemy   give him everything
ever he wanted   give him room   then I will be
king   an earthworm   making things happen   I
will gather my light storm around me   indoors
playing darts against my friends   my enemy   and
the score will go in all directions   in chalk
indoors   or else out on the sidewalk   I guess the
trick to hopscotch remains   all the rhyming
chalk to outline his body   decorated with hair
but first I am trimming his hair   but first I will
brush it

ALL OF THE PEOPLE ARE WALKING

here is certain danger   I can only see the heads
can count them   and won't   there is definitely a
wall   and behind it the heads   *they do not have*
bodies   says one theory   very quietly   I have to
strain to hear it   strain with my head   maybe if I
gave them money   they'd stamp my name on a
brick   I don't know   I meant to get a periscope
I got a microphone instead   would you like to see
it   *hello*   if I'm not mistaken   this thing is on

INSIDE TERMINAL E

the helmet has two purposes   safety and messages
now we are wearing it for safety   hope you feel
better already   anyway   it's not like we are
going to lie down all day on the tarmac   though
we do love the tarmac   it is so responsible and
landed upon   and from it we can count airplane
windows   and clouds won't destroy us   we did
that yesterday   and it's not like we are planning to
repeat ourselves forever   though the messages do
that sometimes

1998

one time this real moon was trying to arrest me   I
was like   *I don't even know what I did wrong*
has the whole world gone away   *why didn't*
anyone tell me   never much good at escape   I
thought I'd try complete surrender   dropped every
weapon I had   then the moon was like   *listen*
you slice of the future   *you can cry but you can't*
make me change

TREATMENT

then people achieved the impossible   and
disappeared   it was like they had gone to live at
Space Camp permanently   we have to envy them
eating freeze-dried ice cream every minute   we
are still here   in the reception area   I understand
if you want to leave   I can wait   I want to help
my goals for this encounter   include for us   to
act like a team   and win

THE ACTUAL FUTURE

I am a handbag   I am the kind of handbag
nobody weeps into   except for when I went to the
ten-year reunion   then everyone wanted to weep
into me   because we have no jobs   and we have
no health insurance   so also we can't have any
babies   now I'm going to talk about the future
of my peer group   the actual future   when I turn
into a human   and have to take vacations to
weep into myself

THANK YOU I WILL SEE MYSELF IN

this room   without which I would fall into space
is useful   it calms me   your face is a room   I
am resting in it   later   refreshed   I will walk
out your mouth   this vase has room for only one
flower   I am an unruly bundle   when I fall down
I take up room   it disappears when not in use   no
I am not using it   do you want to   go ahead
try

HUMAN PROBLEMS

I am in some kind of field   I like it here all the
time swaying   my friend Deirdre came by with an
outfit   *try it on* she said   I always listen when
people start talking   the shirt was beautiful!
pale blue   too large   my head could barely
surpass it   so my friend Deirdre brandished her
little scissors   she said *we can just make a few eye
holes   Deirdre no!*   I said   *stop!   you are
killing me*

OUTNUMBERED

at least one of us is alive   if this is happening
either you are reading   or I am   statistics favor
you   it seems unfair   you get the living hands
or I will object   and kill you   not because I
dislike you   because I like my life   and later
today   in the park   I will only apologize for my
lack of regret   I will eat grapes   I will lie on the
grass   I will have created a little impossibility
that's all I need   a way in   and then to unfold
like a bat

WE MAKE DO

indoors   in the music video   in America   you
are getting warmer   and when you move   your
hair flashes   like a commercial for itself   and my
heart is running   a 100% negative campaign
with irregular beats   I don't mind dying in here
in the light   you are getting warmer   and closer
now   we are both older   and I have cut stars
from envelopes   when we had no night   and
needed night   for the music video   to make sense
in America   at that time   in which you moved
and your hair moved   and all the world followed

PLUS ONE

I lost my phone   I am using the baby monitor
instead   it's in the flowers   nobody's calling
but I know that some day you will   it's just plain
math   love is never more than an extension of
numbers   a cave painting I found   was all plus
signs   it was not a map   it was the greatest
discovery   until I discover my phone   *oh my*
darling   are you ringing   I lost it   it wasn't
hard   like basic math   for instance   guess how
long a person gets to live

POEM CONSISTING ENTIRELY OF ADVICE

you must not look   at what may be a man   or
may be his empty car   what if he asks you   *what
are you looking at*   what if you still do not know

THIS IS CALAMITY HELLO

I know my mind   it gets smaller   like the wide
closing mouth of a cat   there is room for soft
shoes creeping forward   there is room for the no
ones at night   the land that surrounds me has
shifted   one time you were with me   and now
you in a different room   are what   are blinking
are light   I know my eyeballs move   if I press
them   I want to see everything   surely and
wrongly   like a tree without wind thinking   *I'll
just keep moving myself*

AQUALUNG

what I like   likes me back   I like the sky   and
information   I walk around   everything bounces
off the world and sticks to me   and it is called a
system   the red light on my chest   is a symptom
of I am about to be shot   or else I am going to
be mentioned   in a short presentation on love
and deep misgivings   like how today I was
exploring   the pink coral reef   my body slipped
out   and stood beside me   we could not see each
other   and assembled our two visions into one
the world was different   because it looked
different   and it still likes us   but we don't like it
back

CONTINUOUS

I love   you love   he she or it loves   and I wake
up   like a hammer   you wake up   like a quilt
one day we don't wake up at all   it is so funny
we are settled   in our own private tubes   and the
tubes   go reaching up   into the sun   I'd like to
touch you   for a moment   inside the sun   I will
greet you   he she or it will greet you   having
arrived   in the imaginary future   I recognize real
things   like a yolk   and like a fever   those
things   that I can outline all at once   and I do not
lift my pen up from your face

HAPPY BIRTHDAY TO ME

I know where I'm going to die   right here   in my
own honest body   I avoid my body by sleeping
for instance I've just woken up   now here come
my galloping arms   my head the malletless gong
so many days I do not understand   one plows
forward   one gathers   it rains   each month
maintains its own atomic number   a year does not
have a skeleton   it has an uncracked egg   I have
to eat it   I have to get married   my friend the
golden onslaught married stuff in bloom   every
action has a speed and a direction   love goes down
and sometimes slowly   but death can come from
inside or without   for my birthday   I would like
to be an airplane   an airplane with no pilot and no
wings

PARALLELOGRAPH

that is not a bird   that is a large dark area   it is
the same thing   as your head   when I do your
head in silhouette   there could be a nation   that
outlawed the profile   or only thought of outlines
from the front   it is the same as your imaginary
life   you have just given your concession speech
bravely to a small crowd of supporters   they could
be thinking anything and aren't   you can't tell a
large dark area to give up   everything is possible
and not happening   to me in this plausible room
despite the five thousand ways you might reach me
the phone is not ringing   it could be   but it is not
I elect to see but one thing at a time   one broken
toe   one gone-bad sausage   I could possess a
freakish lack of power   like I could be a puncture
but instead I am a vice   it all goes on without   or
else beside me   like in this version of the world
there is no gold

THIS IS NOT THE BODY I ASKED FOR

the thing is   you can't send it back   so   today
I'll accomplish a lot   I will compare my head   to
an eight by twelve glossy photo   of a man on a
fabulous jet-ski   what I see right away is the noise
we both have that in common   I'd like to jet-ski
straight out of this life   because right now I am
way attached to real things   like for instance
people   how they are all so tender   how they
love to just go walk around   and some of them are
wearing pink now   and it hurts me   and they
bathe their dogs

CONDO

microwave doubles as a nightlight   this is that
other song   the one that likes to sing itself   and
stops   microwave has a note   a chord strikes as
light strikes   you can't sleep in it   you might
want to defrost this hunk of beef   I thought
figuratively   there was no beef   there was re-
frigerator   I usually misspell refrigerator
spell-check this hunk of beef   *microwave   what
you rearrange is everything*   that's where heat   a
form of fright   comes from   *welcome to Miami*
came the song   from in the stroller   way down
inside the stroller   sang the man   inside the baby

CHRISTMAS

here is a piece of me   it is my foot   or it is my
spinal attachment   they put a tree in the living
room   of course you'd want to climb it   only the
problem is we are not small enough   and when we
were small enough   we were not strong enough
it wasn't even a question   I do not want this many
parts   I wish I were only one thing   a kneecap
maybe or a liver   if I had a real choice   I would
be an analog phone   then when you were with me
I would keep ringing   and when you kissed me I
would hang up   one man knew how to sing like a
dial tone   I think he was our king   unfortunately
I noticed everything today   and the people won't
let me return it

THEN WE ARE IN AGREEMENT

pick a hand   it has nothing in it   you can keep
my hand as long as you need it   you never know
what a long day this has turned into   you can say
it's only time   but what isn't   maybe if I asked
nicely   you would represent me   in court   in
the future   in many ways   we are alike   we
both have one of my hands   and at least one of us
likes it   I won't speak for you   but am honestly
waiting   in hopes that you might speak for me
make statements   deny statements   the vital
thing's to make a little noise

LINE UP IN AN ORDERLY FASHION

a disaster moving toward me   must first fill out
the forms   then I will cry for nine days   I will
make two extra copies   friends   there are no
limits to my understanding   I understand my head
off   *miss*   they say to me   *miss*   but I can't
hear a thing   over the noise of breaking pencils
and outlines and waves   love or hate the ocean
you still drown like other sailors   getting wet
getting wet   getting wet

WHERE I AM AT

now I am in your television   with my co-star
Terrible Need   Terrible Need is a legend to work
with   we have a great time on the set   I learned a
lot from her   how to move a body through space
she calls it *getting delivered*   a lot of the time we
have food delivered   of course   we don't
actually eat it   it's not that kind of show   it is a
show about two talented hens   on a long and wet
island   the island hangs around us   like a frame

GOOD LUCK EVERYONE

hunger has the man   purchase a bun   the man
eats the bun   then he has no bun   and no hunger
the man lives in Illinois   hunger has the shape
of a different state   a square one   one hunger is
much like another   and in the park   similar
statues don't move   in a similar way   is anyone
hungry   has hunger prompted anyone   to wander
slowly across state lines   in search of food   and
tracking one kind of soil   on top of another   in
the book the man is reading   there is a tree-based
society   the women and the men   all live in trees
the man gets confused   between sticks   and
jokes about sticks   each one goes   and then it
ends   but they are different

CATALOGUE

there was a hole   in my hands   I was holding it
it was hard   it was an old hole   *you do not
belong* I said to the hole   I took some action
typed up the headline   *to whom*   then typed up
the body   *does this belong*   it was hard   with
the hole in my hands   I could not manage   I set
it beside me   there were eighteen responses   one
part said   *not to me*   the other part was silent
the hole did not look sad   it didn't look like
anything   that is how I came to lose it   I reported
my loss   in return   I got several feelings   there
were nine   they were refurbished feelings

TRYING TO MAKE A DIFFERENCE

to more readily know where you stop   surround
yourself with water   a short cruise   a headcount
you go first   now we will with luck avoid
everything   *hello empty landscape   flat arena*
it is nice   there are no walls to run into   like that
man from *Singing in the Rain*   one thing you don't
want   is to be like other people   you want to
launch sideways   with nothing to stop you   let's
swim around until by chance   we dance the same
maneuvers   let's check in   in eighteen hundred
months

A GLASS OF SALT WATER

when one boat overtakes another   on television
there is somebody watching   and also there is
another person steering the first boat   and I'll let
you fill in the rest   the ocean is already full   but
people keep adding to it anyway   the way you
might to a painting   it needs a little more flair
people take sardines out of the ocean   but are not
above returning them   in cans   that can't see us
so far as we know   no one should put me in
charge of a boat   or regatta   I fear that my world
might tip over   you must always leave a tip
even if the service is awful   she could be in the midst
of some crisis   or she could be your mother

OUR SENSE OF ACHIEVEMENT

trees do not mean to cause us harm   trees move
themselves across the planet   in wide invisible
lines   trees are all around us like fire   once there
was a song called   *Everything We Know About
Chairs*   but nobody wrote it   where would you
even begin   every day many things do not happen
a perfect love   a perfect winter   you don't fail
once   you keep failing   just when you think
you've got it right   arrives some spring

ABOUT A WHALE

I look like my baby   I haven't had my baby   my
baby is a feeling   I have about myself   look I am
all alone   in the living room   you don't know
this   but it's completely different   it is nighttime
everywhere   even Cameroon   there is a song for
every feeling   there are not so many feelings   the
song for this feeling   is the one about a whale

KINDS OF WEATHER

I got so mad   when I died   in a balloon   with
all my hope   there were people blanketing the
earth   like placemats   I loved those people
they were wheat to me   they sustained me   but I
couldn't show it   I was so mad   and I was dead
it's not normal   for a person   to be contained in a
basket   aloft in blank air   like water in a red cup
I took the shape of my death   and my anger
there was no forgiveness   there were so many
clouds   and I punched them   stratocumulus
cumulonimbus   they were just pieces of water   I
looked down at all the people   they were units
they shifted around   they clumped up   into little
factions   there was no way to join them   from
the balloon   nothing would become of me now   I
moved my face to the basket   started chewing   I
chewed the air   until there wasn't enough to still
name it   I ate up the earth   ate up those people
and then I was nowhere   and they could not save
me

SPRING POEM FOR HARPO

if we did not have skin   we would not have
gladness   skin is what keeps the gladness in   you
know you are glad when the skin begins swelling
you can almost not contain it   the gladness   the
feeling when you touch a warm stone with all five
of your toes   then the others   the sun will one
day grow   so glad it will destroy us   our skin
an immense gladness will go all over   all
humming   like it is a farmer   to dwell upon this
planet is a radical consolation   already I am
swelling up   like a berry   not smartly   in a two
foot patch of   look no snow

THE PLAN

we must stop taking for granted   the demented
look   the trees have adopted   despite our
pleading   we did not plead at all   what were we
doing   sorting buttons   braiding each other's
long quiet hair   the trees all the time grow
stronger   it's hard enough   to look at them   let
alone sketch them   with our mere hands   mere
ink   mere eraser   fuck it   let's become
caterpillars   or uncontrollable blazes   let's go set
ourselves alight

LANDSCAPING

I have to love the baby   with the gold car   in his
mouth   I have to love the grass   the grass   the
asphalt   I just make up the rules   and then I obey
them   I have to fall   back up into my tree   like
an envelope   not enough postage   it's a sign   I
should never try again   I have to love town lines
they are always very funny   you can move the
baby   back and forth   between them   almost
nothing is a toy   if you don't use it   use the baby
a baby brightens   any yard in which it's placed

LIFE VEST

is it safe now to say   Canada's no longer funny
no   it is not safe   to say anything   because your
mouth could detach   and sail away   to an openly
new continent   I don't know   in the Pacific
precautions are stupid   they eat into our limited
budget   nobody takes my sweater off   ever   I
have feelings too   and at night   when my cat eats
my hair   that is also a feeling   the way a nation
is   persistent   the way you can wake up
feeling Canadian   even after you are dead

THINGS WE MIGHT TRY

everybody go home   everybody step out   I want
the real world   to look like it's blinking   I can't
make it happen alone   everybody get on the
automatic sidewalk   now we are relatively still
and want the brief world   to look like it's passing
to see the woman in the green shirt   against the
green leaves   and then the green leaves are white
siding   now a yellow van has arrived   we have
so much to work with   so much to arrange   like
rocks and like all the new widows   I understand
two categories   one of objects   the other of force
we want the wind   to come in   and erase things
against what   would we look like ourselves   if
we stick our heads   through these holes   then
you are a shellfish and I am a pun   and we are out
three or four bucks   but everyone   I will pay you
back   just as soon   as we all make a fist   I
mean one fist   I want it to last

I KNOW THE AIR SHOULD NOT CONTAIN ME

I am on a plane   I am trying to distract myself
imagining some other face at hand   the tree
honestly exploding at the tips   or a necessity   a
drugstore   an anything   only I don't want to
think of dead men's shirts   out drying and waving
on the line   so I think of the sun   I think about
hammers   I put a long green field in my head
and I put it below me   she's bringing me peanuts
I think about peanuts   not about silence   I
arrange my records alphabetically   by the first
word   of the first song   and the first word is
constantly *baby*   among the corn   I place an
outlet for the farmer if he needs it   and none of
this cares for me   I stare and stare at a coupon
and the coupon just will not stare back   *where are*
we going   I ask no one out loud   and kindly
nobody replies   and I am not hungry   I love to
be hungry   with room for a whole life inside
and damn all these freezing old counties   their
hundred receipts and their corners   if I fell from
here   I'd live on as a dull yellow quadrangle
and I would keep heaving in sun   but I'm eating
ice   flying over our shadow   I am leaving every
coast   every tide pool   where I was born   and
where I dipped my feet in   I am separating clouds
from sky   not harmed   not in flames   in the
undisclosed heart of my nation

·

WHAT YOU WILL

have painted this room   so many times   there is
hardly space left to stand up in   small mistakes
repeated over time   that is how I am a system
who will be the head of this department   who will
let me out to feed the mule   all the time the skin
it works so hard to contain things   and I want to
say thank you   I want to remember   I am trying
to move faster   through my life   toward that tree
which does not care   and skin does not care
velocity won't make me feel special   who will tilt
my chin up   to the angle where he wants me
who will leave my building falling down

DEMANDS SATISFACTION

I am only one piece of the rabble   on Sundays I
don't go out anymore   I assemble what limbs need
assembly   the rabble are trembling   I mean the
trees always look like that   only this time I want to
kick my own legs about   kick up some stars
pull the night down   over my technical head   it
is always morning   the rabble still asleep and
breathing   when I thought   the other day   I
thought of what I could do in his sleep   and I did
not mean dreams   I meant how one goes out
walking   one follows who knows what   and
never arrives   if I could simply get up   I could
hang upside down   from that tree   there   the
one to which I'm pointing   and I could dry out
shaking   if the wind came   I think that it would

SOUP IS ONE FORM OF SALT WATER

I am making borscht   please do not laugh at me
I seem to have ruined my soul   the quality of
television programming grows stronger all the time
soon we will live in the ocean   we will all return
to the ocean   my hands are bright pink   like I
have been applauding you for hours   my love for
you is louder than I know   I saw a show last night
there were four thousand brides left in Iceland   I
was laughing   but it was not funny   the brides
looked embarrassed   and cold   I must not wash
anywhere but a tidepool   I must use starfish to
scrub at my hands   I am writing this to say   I am
not leaving you forever   I am going to get better
and then I'll come home

MOVING OUT

goodbye slow world   you know who you are
and I am not going to tell you it's okay   because it
might change your behavior   and change is the
single value I've assigned   I like this house better
with nothing in it   *hello*   it helps me if we stop
paying attention   one foot after one foot   and
before you know it   we are still here

TRYING TO RETURN THE SUN

I don't need anything   but you and some light
the world goes on   getting inferred   it is so
stubborn   and will not erase things   I think I
should scrub out my eyes   you will recognize me
still   won't you   I am much older now   older
than I'll ever be   all these eyes in my head   and
the light   what distinguishes my face from a tree
is the total lack of commentary   as in that tree
loves you   honestly loves you   I'm the noisy one
who has to say it

WHAT WE HAVE WORKED FOR

you were holding me when the tulips collapsed
we had not given them the water   I was holding
the water in my hands   and you were holding me
when I fell to the wavering ground   and for the
tulips we are not sorry   oh no   we're not sorry at
all   the water is clean and warm   and sustains us
up to our knees   any moment now   we'll start to
blossom   my head will crack open   and fall
through your hands   oh hands cannot keep
anything together pretty baby   oh it beats me why
we try

ACKNOWLEDGMENTS

Sincere thanks to the editors of the following journals, where many of these poems, or earlier versions of them, first appeared.

6X6, 751, Agricultural Reader, The Awl, Black Warrior Review, Boston Review, Dewclaw, Fence, Fou, Gulf Coast, Jellyroll, La Petite Zine, Madison Review, New Orleans Review, No: a journal of the arts, Octopus, Skein, and Slope.

...

Thank you to the following people for their generous help with the making of these poems and this book:

Chris DeWeese, Jess Fjeld, Lisa Olstein, Zach Schomburg, Mathias Svalina, Jim Tate, Emily Toder, and Dara Wier.

Thank you to Emory University and the University of Massachusetts Amherst, whose support gave me time to work.

The epigraph is taken from Aleksandar Ristović's poem, "Daydreaming in the midst of spring labors," as translated by Charles Simic.

"When the Sun Went Down They Kept Growing" is for Amanda Nadelberg.